Pray for Potatoes:

Pursue Professional Success Through God's Love

Pray for Potatoes:

Pursue Professional Success Through God's Love

Rovina Broomfield

Pray for Potatoes: Pursue Professional Success Through God's Love

Published by MacKenzie Publishing
Halifax, Nova Scotia
ISBN-13: 978-1-927529-56-0
ISBN-10: 1927529565
September 2018

Cover designer: Marla Bonner of Modify Marla Design
www.modifymarla.com
@modifymarla

Edited by C.A. MacKenzie

Note: Some scripture quotations are paraphrased by the author.

MacKenzie Publishing

Contents

Introduction

Employees in most corporations quickly learn the power of a title within their functions and across teams. Typically, entry-level positions start with an associate title and progress upward in responsibility and power, with titles such as manager, senior manager, director, and vice president.

Motivated individuals realize the importance of a career growth plan, which usually describes their pursuit of the next title. It is easy for us to become focused on promotion and recognition if we orient our careers around the pursuit of the highest corporate title.

Set aside corporate titles, center your eyes on God, and consider the most significant title necessary in your career. If you were already at the top of the ranks, how would that change the way you walk into the office? How would you lead your next meeting? How would you give feedback to your manager? As you read this book, begin to realize that you already have the most meaningful and powerful professional title—Child of God. In a corporation, the leader who sets the vision and mission for the company is the owner, and as children of Christ, God is our CEO.

Matthew 6:33 reads: "But seek first His kingdom and His righteousness, and all these things will be given to you as well." The instruction is clear. Be careful what you seek, where you focus your mind, and where you put your energy because those thoughts will become your reality.

Here, I narrow the focus on what we seek professionally because the world has a loud message of misdirection on how to become successful and how to manage the successes and failures in your career. No matter what professional level you find yourself in today—entry-level to senior leader—your focus should remain unchanged as a Child of God. That level of discipline is one of the greatest challenges of our lives.

I have practiced the strategies outlined in this book for several years, and I'm convinced doing so keeps my mind at peace and my decision-making sharp. I also want to clarify any misconceptions you may have up front. This is not a guide to becoming a rich and famous CEO, nor is it the key to landing a dream job.

This is a guide to keep you focused on your pursuit of God's love, His plan, and His will. There will be failures and losses on the road ahead and on the path to victory. My prayer for you is to use these strategies as methods to deal with the let-downs along with the huge wins in your professional life.

Regardless of the circumstance, your title as Child of God has been freely given to you. It is yours without having to earn a related degree, apply for the position, or attend a performance review. Even still, it gets better! With God as your CEO, you are on a business team that cannot fail long-term.

Success is a promise that will be fulfilled in His time (Ecclesiastes 3:11). That can be hard to fully accept because you first must believe that His time matters above all. Then erase your definition of success and replace it with the understanding that He has clearly defined success for your life. Accepting those two things can be difficult for everyone, including me.

To release your timelines and trust God's definition of success are difficult because we are taught to set goals using those exact parameters—time-bound and measurable. Unfortunately, those constraints do not matter to God. He gives us what we need when we need it. Trust His plans for you to be successful because He's a good, good Father. Your responsibility is to remain disciplined and perform well in your uniquely designed role for the sake of His corporation, which is the Body of Christ. I get goosebumps thinking about the promises of God for my life, my career, my family, my legacy. You should too. It's here for all of us.

Living up to this sizable level of responsibility is hard to imagine until you realize the Bible contains the instruction we need to succeed and flourish. The goal of this book is to equip you with the tools—scriptures, prayers, and confessions—to stay grounded in grace and truth while progressing in the corporate environment.

I am convinced you are called to be a leader. To meet this calling, you must have a foundation rooted in a relationship with God and an unwavering focus on seeking His Kingdom.

Chapter 1

Pray that hearts are softened for you.

In most companies, there is a hierarchy, an Org Chart, to indicate decision-making power and authority. While respect for authority is important, you must also understand that as a Child of God you have authority granted through another source. The key to proper use of our Father's authority is to learn our Father's heart. Then you will begin to see the world and the people in it with His lens of love.

One step you can follow at work—and in life in general—that gets you closer to His view is to concern yourself with the condition of the hearts of your colleagues and business partners.

When you first read "the condition of the heart," you may think every heart is essentially the same red, pulsating, blood-pumping organ. Kind of beautiful and kind of scary-looking but consistent person to person.

If you think a bit harder about what you learned in school, you may recall lessons explaining how to have a healthy heart. Lessons about eating grains and working out to have a strong heart and live a long life. That should trigger the memory of learning that hearts can be weak or strong, and of course, you want a strong heart. Who doesn't? Strong is generally better than weak. That's a concept we can get behind.

Take it a step further and reference the biblical descriptions of the condition of one's heart to understand how significant the heart is to humanity. When you use the Bible to understand the heart, you learn another dimension of the heart. God describes the condition of the heart as binary, hard or soft, evil or love.

Through scripture, you and I learn the hard heart is disobedient to the instructions of God. A person with a hard heart can be angered quickly, be an irrational decision-maker, or be condescending in feedback to others.

One with a soft heart is open to receive the word of God and to follow His guidance. A colleague with a soft heart listens, looks for opportunities to uplift others, and communicates directly without being mean-spirited.

The challenge and opposition from a hardened heart can feel discouraging and unreasonable to people with soft hearts. Through the challenge, first remember you are not to live in fear or intimidation. Instead, when you face a hard heart, pray for an improved condition and continue to love them with your positive disposition. You and I will face hard hearts, and sometimes they are not meant to change in that season. In fact, sometimes hard hearts are in your life for a reason and to teach a necessary lesson in your development.

When you are up against a challenging personality, don't fall into the temptation to battle them with their style of communication. Remember God as your CEO, and then embrace the authority you walk in each day and be aware of your role as an influencer in your environment.

I once read, "The same boiling water that hardens the egg softens the potato." At first, I thought it meant that I needed to respond differently to the circumstances of my life. I could choose to be an egg and get hardened by life, or I could choose to be a potato and soften up and enjoy things. Then, during an evening of Bible reading and prayer, I realized you and I weren't the eggs or the potatoes; we were the water.

As a Christian and a child of the highest God, you should always be the boiling water—boiling should be your standard temperature. God tells us a very clear warning about being lukewarm water. The scripture reads, "So, because you are lukewarm—neither hot nor cold—I am about to spit you out of my mouth." (Revelations 3:16). To be lukewarm, in between hot and cold, is not an acceptable state of being. God calls us to be decisive and definite. In your faith and in your career, it is best to be on fire for what you believe in. You and I must constantly be reminded of the importance of being on fire for God and on fire with His love for others. As you work on getting closer to God and building a personal relationship with Him, you will begin to boil with passion and energy for the vision ahead of your life. That is when your faith and connection to God will move you so that boiling water is your natural state.

Then, the people you encounter will either be eggs or potatoes, and their state is determined by the condition of their heart. When you become aware of these roles in your workplace, you should also accept the responsibility to pray for potatoes to enter your presence and for their hearts to soften to your ideas and solutions.

If you are anything like me, you want to be the best at your job and you want other people at work to acknowledge your awesomeness. This is not from a position of vanity or because you seek validation, but from a desire for appreciation and reputation-building. While I have worked hard my entire life—as a student, athlete, employee, and now as a creator and entrepreneur—the appreciation and reputation I seek are not based solely on my own performance.

I wish for my team to be a highly sought-after group within the company, and I hope for my employees to be known as high-potential leaders in other teams and organizations. To achieve these goals, I aim to work well with others to get the best out of everyone. Most often, you will work in a team environment of competition and collaboration, and that requires a balanced approach of being your best self and building up those around you.

I remember learning a life-changing lesson in my early twenties. As I transitioned from student life into the corporate world, I realized the magnitude others had on the opportunities afforded to me. I was a twenty-three-year-old with a master's in business administration. Someone would have to take a risk to believe I could be a master at anything, right? Although I landed a job at a great company, it wasn't the job I desired. It was not a role that valued—or compensated—my MBA. I was bummed.

This was the first time my hard work was not enough to get me the outcome I had planned. After about a year, I was ready to try again to reach my professional goal. The jobs I applied to did not work out. More rounds of rejection. Then a recruiter I met months prior reached out to me about a new opportunity. I was curious, we chatted, and I was convinced to apply.

This time, when I landed my first-round phone interview, I changed my preparation strategy. Instead of focusing my pre-interview prayers on myself and my abilities, I prayed exclusively for my interviewer to be in a good mood, enjoy the conversation with me, and believe in my abilities.

Before this instance, I used to add a quick few seconds of prayer for the interviewers at the last minute, just to check the box. It was always difficult for me to commit to praying for the interviewer because I was accustomed to focusing on myself during those final moments leading up to the interview. To spend time praying for others when my success was on the line was illogical to me. I thought, *Why would I spend my time praying for them? I need to pray for myself. Pray for me to have the right answers and to say the right things.*

This time was different. It was the first time I committed myself to pray for the interviewer, but it was not because I realized it was the right thing to do. To be honest, I wanted this role, and I was so nervous I decided to try a new approach. I was seeking a winning strategy, and this seemed a reasonable idea that could only make things better, so why not commit to it?

That first interview was not easy. I wouldn't call it a slam dunk, but it went okay. I prayed for the interviewer again immediately after the call ended. When I got an email about a second-round phone interview the next day, I was convinced praying for the interviewer was my new strategy.

About a month later, I quit my job and moved across the country to start a new career with the opportunity and growth potential I had desired for a year and a half. The total interview process involved about seven interviewers, and I prayed for each one before I met them. I realized a successful interview was not only about what I said but also about how I was heard and what was retained. I needed God's help with that.

I truly believe it was my prayer for potatoes—soft hearts and positive attitudes—that opened doors for me. God says He will change the condition of our hearts, so I called out to Him to do so (Ezekiel 36:26). Yes, I was a risky candidate, and I was told by peers that I was overshooting. I needed soft hearts along the way to receive the right opportunities in corporate environments. Praying for soft hearts was my secret weapon to earn a great job that provided me with significant increases in finances and responsibilities. I have carried that lesson with me every step of my career.

You and I are compared to peers for annual reviews and bonus assessments at work, and these assessments can happen more frequently depending on the company structure. Your employee rating is not merely a matter of how well you performed, but rather who vouched for you. What do they remember about you? How does the leadership feel when they hear your name or see your profile on the screen when making evaluations? This is why I pray for soft hearts, and you should too.

My prayers concerning the conditions of the hearts of others started as a calming strategy for interview prep to focus on others and to make the process less about me. I am grateful for the lesson I learned as a byproduct about the importance of praying for others. As Christians, a substantial amount of our prayer power should be used to pray for other people when we use Jesus as an example of how much we should love and care for others. I have heard this commitment to others described as "standing in the gap" for the people in our lives, rather than inwardly focused on our own needs and desires.

I encourage you to pray over your work environment boldly each day. When you look at your calendar and meeting schedule, pray one sentence for each meeting—the attendees, the subject, the outcome—and see how your focus and effectiveness in meetings improve. You should call on God to enter spaces where you spend your time even before you arrive. This helps reveal the right places to be and will move the right people in or out of those spaces with you.

Of course, let me also acknowledge that reality doesn't always turn out as you asked in prayers. If it did, we'd all be prayer warriors! When the outcome is not what I prayed for and not my desire or leaves me disappointed or sad, I pray out loud to thank God for peace and patience. That is when we are tested to trust in God's plan above our own (Isaiah 55:8-9; Philippians 4:4-7).

There are instances where God intentionally hardens the hearts of people to teach lessons in faith or as preparation for the future. Remind yourself that God's timing is perfect timing. When you experience moments of disappointment and sadness, first recognize that God can place a hard heart in your path intentionally as He did with the hard heart of the pharaoh with Moses in the book of Exodus.

Remain calm and still with your presence centered on God and you will be sustained (Isaiah 40:31). Call to God to reveal a vision of progress and resolve to you in a new way. Thank Him for the opportunity to grow and build the strength you need to achieve your greater purpose beyond the challenge of the present.

I often find myself repeating the phrase, "Not my time, God; Your time. It's not my time, God; it's Your time." This mantra serves as a simple reminder to trust in Him and to continue to strive for His plan to guide my life. He has a purpose for you.

The pursuit of purpose is a tricky one. It is motivating to know you and I are called to do something awesome for our world, but it can cause us to rely on ourselves too much at the expense of others. The world teaches you to fight for the first position, to take success by defeating others because we can't all win together. This is a misdirection.

To resist these negative thoughts as your career progresses, focus your prayers outward and continue to pray that hearts are softened for you during highs and lows. With God as your CEO, you understand opportunity and success is here for all of us and it is your commitment to His plan that gets you to your place at the right time. He promises His children abundant lives (John 10:10)—not some of us, all of us. You and I will have different paths toward our abundance, so trust in His plan and path for your life. Amid the discouragement and doubt that will creep into your mind, be a seeker of the Kingdom, continue to move forward, and do not look backward.

What does it mean to be a seeker of the Kingdom? It means to focus on the Kingdom of Heaven as your ultimate destination and find resolve in God through all circumstances. When you need to make a difficult decision, solve a challenging problem, or lead a high-intensity meeting, the right choices and words come to you if you give it to God. Own the preparation and be on fire for the task ahead so that you are boiling water, and in the few minutes of preparation before you take position, remind yourself that He is the one in control.

"Take delight in the Lord, and He will give you the desires of your heart." (Psalm 37:4). The blessings and plans of God do not always come easily or on the first try. The stories of men and women in the Bible reveal examples of faith and obedience necessary through trials and tribulations. As a Child of God, your success comes with endurance, and you'll need soft hearts along the way for opportunities and resources to be granted. Do your part to first be boiling water, and then pray for others and for their hearts to be softened toward you.

Focus Scriptures

Read these scriptures to be reminded of how hearts are softened for you.

Revelations 3:16 *So, because you are lukewarm—neither hot nor cold—I am about to spit you out of my mouth.*

Ezekiel 36:26 *I will give you a new heart and put a new spirit in you; I will remove from you your heart of stone and give you a heart of flesh.*

Isaiah 55:8-9 *For my thoughts are not your thoughts, neither are your ways my ways," declares the Lord. "As the heavens are higher than the earth, so are my ways higher than your ways and my thoughts than your thoughts.*

Philippians 4:4-7 *Rejoice in the Lord always. I will say it again: Rejoice! Let your gentleness be evident to all. The Lord is near. Do not be anxious about anything, but in every situation, by prayer and petition, with thanksgiving, present your requests to God. And the peace of God, which transcends all understanding, will guard your hearts and your minds in Christ Jesus.*

Isaiah 40:31 *But those who hope in the Lord will renew their strength. They will soar on wings like eagles; they will run and not grow weary, they will walk and not be faint.*

John 10:10 *The thief comes only to steal and kill and destroy; I have come that they may have life, and have it to the full.*

Psalm 37:4 *Take delight in the Lord, and he will give you the desires of your heart.*

Confession

Recite this prayer out loud when praying for hearts to be softened to you.

God, I pray that You soften the hearts of the leaders on my team and at my company. Allow them to lead with a spirit of love and kindness toward one another. Not in a way that weakens us, instead one that gives opportunity and opens doors for those prepared to walk through them, Father. Let me speak the right words and be remembered fondly as a strong mind and refreshing energy. When selections are made for increase and opportunity, Lord, let my name be spoken without hesitation.

God, renew the minds and hearts in my workplace. As decisions need to be made and problems solved, let me turn to You for resolutions. Be my source of navigation. Let me start each day delighting myself in You and Your grace.

Chapter 2

See people. Care enough to create community.

Have you ever imagined what life would be like if you were born into the Royal Family in the United Kingdom? While I certainly would not describe myself as a girly-girl, even I have imagined life as a princess.

I imagine it being glamorous, with access to any and every possession around the world simply by telling someone my name. The status that would come with my family's royal name would be of the highest regard across many lands. Maybe you think how cool it would be to call your favorite celebrity your best friend. You'd hang out, walk around the biggest city streets, and go to the most exclusive parties because of whom you know.

You and I can easily imagine scenarios when access is granted because of our association. This is exactly what God has in mind for you as His child.

When you learn you are a Child of God and understand you are always more than enough (2 Corinthians 9:8) to achieve the plan for your life, you should become excited to grow closer with and become more like your co-heir, Christ (Romans 8:17). Take a moment and let that sink in—you are co-heirs with Christ, arguably the most influential and talked about person to ever walk the earth—that's an amazing family name to be a part of.

As co-heirs, you and I inherited the same power and authority that Jesus possessed while walking the earth. When you look at how Jesus used His power, you will find countless examples of Him doing good things for others and being a beacon of hope and renewal for individuals who have experienced great failure or loss.

Be honest with yourself, have you ever looked around during your daily commute or in the office kitchen to see if someone needs hope or renewal?

Even more impressive than Jesus' kindness is His humility and empathy. Unfortunately, it seems human nature guides us to optimize for selfishness. When you gain power and status without established habits to resist those natural temptations, you risk allowing that desire to propel and defend yourself to become dominant in your thoughts and actions. As co-heirs with Christ, after you gain power and authority in the workplace, you must also be diligent to make room for less of you and more of Him in your daily life. This is the strategy you should develop as early as possible in your career. It will be what sets you apart in the long-term from others who also have positions of authority but are not using it for the good of others.

The marked ability to perform over others can cause some to lose humility and succumb to the temptations of their flesh. We see this often from political leaders and celebrities. We hear how money changed someone or how leaders find themselves committing acts they would never have imagined in order to protect self and personal wants.

When you look to the Bible for instructions to manage power and status, the life of Jesus, an incredible example, is the model for you. Amidst many miracles and powerful displays, He remained humble and gracious. He models how to balance success on earth with submission to God's will, and was able to resist human temptations and pitfalls that accompany authority. That balance is one you and I should pursue in our own lives.

Consider how often Jesus stopped during His journeys to talk with others and willingly engaged in conversations with the outcasts of society. It was neither social status nor wealth that made people visible to Him; it was compassion and empathy that drew Jesus to people. Furthermore, He did more than see people. He valued them and called them to great roles and responsibilities in their communities.

Great leaders are distinguished by an ability to identify the strengths and needs of others and then guide and position them to be at their best. People want to be seen, valued, appreciated, and rewarded.

To develop this ability, you must form the habit to pause and sincerely connect with those around you. The habits you establish at the beginning when handling small responsibilities will sustain you throughout the phases of your career challenges and expansion.

I suggest three steps to develop this area:

1. Acknowledge each day that your surroundings were uniquely designed for you;

2. Appreciate God's perfect plan and realize each person you cross paths with was intended; and

3. Slow down to experience the small moments in your day.

First, take a moment to acknowledge that your surroundings were uniquely designed for you. Thank God for guiding your steps before you step out of bed each morning, which flows directly into an appreciation of His plan for your life.

Imagine for a moment that each person you cross paths with is an intentional cross section planned by God. As in movies, there are main characters, accessory characters, and extras written into the scripts of our lives.

Look back at the last year of your life. Have the main characters changed? Look at the last five people you've called. Does that list look the same as it did twelve months ago? Odds are high the answer is no, because the chapter of your life has changed. The essential characters from one chapter can sometimes become nonexistent in the next chapter. That same character placement happens every day in your work environment. You should value the moments you have with each person. Look at the cast of characters around you. Why they have been placed there?

The last step to begin to build the habit of seeing others is to slow down and experience the small moments of your day. Avoid the sense of urgency that is far too commonly embraced, along with distraction and inward attention. The smallest interaction—eye contact, a smile, holding the door—is an opportunity to display God's love.

When you enter the office building, it is easy to walk with your head down and immediately begin to focus inward to prepare for the agenda ahead of you. However, with God as your CEO, that is not who you were designed to be.

You could be a colleague's first example of a person displaying the love of Christ. Perhaps your kindness and patience will be their first encounter with Jesus. When you consider that unique opportunity, you should want to be intentional with human interactions and find it easier to resist the screen time and selfish thoughts as you pass through the workday.

To achieve this level of awareness for others, you must slow down, look up, and see those planted in your presence. Don't rush through spaces with your head down or enter an elevator and immediately pull out your phone. Keep your head up, greet people with a smile, and say hello. From that brief greeting flows positivity. Let God's peace and calm flow through you and into your surroundings.

In my office buildings, I make it a point to speak to the building staff—security guards, maintenance crew, and janitorial staff—in addition to my colleagues. I appreciate conversations that allow me to learn about their families, hobbies, vacations, and their heritage in the city. Along with my appreciation to learn, these chats are a great break in my workday to recharge my brain. If I'm in a hurry, it may be a nod, a smile, or a wave, but I let people know I see them. My steps are ordered by the Lord (Psalm 37:23), so I value those in my path.

You and I must believe that God places everyone intentionally along our journey. When you consider that interaction was scripted in God's plan, does that change how you would behave in that moment? If so, adopt the behavior change now and start developing the right habits of seeing people.

You and I are here to see people, to be engaged enough to be aware of their heart's condition, and to gesture—small or grand—to acknowledge their presence. Contrary to the instincts of corporate America, greetings and kind words should not be reserved only when seeking approval. It's our role to see all people as God's children and as valuable people on our paths each day.

After you hone your ability to truly see people, the next level of development is to create a welcoming and flourishing community amongst your colleagues. You will find that you care for your community and its wholeness above yourself. This is when you are truly living as a co-heir and a living reflection of God in your world. The instruction from your CEO is simple: whenever there is an opportunity to reflect less of yourself and more of Him, do it.

We are called to be the "light of the world" and the "salt of the earth" (Matthew 5:13-16). That is a huge calling and responsibility placed on you when you recognize yourself as a Child of God. On our planet, light will always displace darkness, and salt adds immense value to life through flavor and preservation. That comparison is the amount of impact God desires you to carry into the spaces you enter and to share with those around you.

In addition to people you cross paths with once, you have colleagues or "regulars" you expect to see and build relationships with over time. You have an added responsibility to the regulars, which is to speak positive words over them and to express sincere interest in their well-being. The saying, "teamwork makes the dream work," is one of my favorite mantras when I enter the office, and I aim to cultivate that collaborative spirit on my business teams. The team functions best when all of its members believe in the goals and the mission of the group. When you notice someone losing momentum or motivation, it is important to create the space through a trusted relationship to find out why.

Before you can commit to see people and engage with them in personal conversations, you should become comfortable with being uncomfortable. You will not be able to relate to all people or all experiences, but that does not prevent you from offering your time to listen and express sincere care for their well-being. God will give you what you need in those moments—the words to say or the ears to hear. You'd be surprised how much individuals hold inside with the desire to discuss but find themselves silenced by the fear of judgment, negative labels, or social exclusion based on their story. As a Child of God, knowing He came for all of us, you should live a life filled with grace to pour out into the world.

As you experience professional success, you will receive an increased authority and influence over others, along with more ownership of the work environment. While the basic thought of professional success sounds good to you, it may sound daunting to imagine being the CEO of a company. However, that senior level position becomes realistic when you begin to expect growth in your authority and influence. Both are the results of your ability to effectively lead and see people as God sees them.

It is important to maintain humility as your scope of leadership expands, and I've found that comes with an assertive resistance to the worldly depiction of climbing the ladder of success. Too often, the corporate world defines this climb as a series of head-to-head battles, each with a victor and a fallen opponent. Thus, the more ambitious employees in the office are taught to take pride in counting fallen opponents as achievement measures. This constant battle culture is detrimental to a team because it creates division and will be in conflict with productive teamwork.

As a leader, you should be aware and alert to eliminate the battle culture people can be tempted to fall into at work. I will touch more on that in the pages to come. Such a culture will damage your ability to influence and can separate you from your team if they perceive you as a blocker on their paths to success rather than a builder and supporter.

Care about the individuals on your team and about the whole team as a single unit. Be curious and interested in their lives outside of work and their overall happiness. A key to being authentic when getting to know colleagues is to thank God for the people in your path, recognize those people are placed according to His plan, and ask God to slow you down.

Focus Scriptures

Read these scriptures to be reminded of how to see people and create community.

2 Corinthians 9:8 *And God is able to bless you abundantly, so that in all things at all times, having all that you need, you will abound in every good work.*

Romans 8:17 *Now if we are children, then we are heirs—heirs of God and co-heirs with Christ, if indeed we share in his sufferings in order that we may also share in his glory.*

Psalm 37:23 *The Lord makes firm the steps of the one who delights in him;*

Matthew 5:13-16 *"You are the salt of the earth. But if the salt loses its saltiness, how can it be made salty again? It is no longer good for anything, except to be thrown out and trampled underfoot.*
"You are the light of the world. A town built on a hill cannot be hidden. Neither do people light a lamp and put it under a bowl. Instead they put it on its stand, and it gives light to everyone in the house. In the same way, let your light shine before others, that they may see your good deeds and glorify your Father in heaven.

Confession

Recite this prayer out loud when praying to see people and create community.

God, let me see people as Jesus sees them. We all matter, and we're all co-heirs with Jesus. Let me see those I interact with as brothers and sisters. Give me the patience to look them in the eye, sincerely ask how they're doing, and listen for their response. I pray the people in my community and sphere of influence are excited to see me, God, because they see You in me.

Each day, let there be less of me and more of You. I ask that You speak through me when someone needs to hear Your love. God, keep my eyes open and my heart clean. I thank You for giving me Your Spirit to walk with each day.

Chapter 3

Ask God to manage the relationships in your life.

The relationships you accept will influence the person you become. This is true in work and in your personal life.

Growing up, I thought about personal relationships in terms of emotional influence. As a child, I would decide if a person made me happy or sad, and if they hurt me, I did not want to be friends with them. That was a daily decision on the playground as a preschooler. Over time, as I matured and relationships became increasingly complex, it was difficult to know what role or influence someone should have in my life. There were times I positioned people incorrectly and the outcome was confusion or regret. In early adulthood, as I grew in my relationship with God, I learned strategies to position people in my life to minimize the negative outcomes.

New people enter your spaces often. Some are there for brief passing periods and others for a longer purpose. You should put a great deal of consideration into those you call friends because of the influence they will have on your evolution as a Child of God. Although He is the almighty ruler, God gave you and me free will. With free will comes an abundance of daily choices, big and small. When you isolate the decisions made at work, you should be able to confidently say it is your relationship with God that is leading you. When you choose a team to join or a new hire to bring onto your team, discuss the decision specifically with God and be patient for His reply.

The first time I turned a relationship over to God was in the midst of personal turmoil. However, I now take that approach to both personal and professional relationships. During this time in my early twenties, I was in a troubled personal relationship. One night, I found myself on my knees in prayer at the side of my bed, feeling weak. In that moment, I realized I could not make the decision on my own to keep this person in my life or let go and accept their season had passed. Overwhelmed and conflicted, I surrendered the relationship to God, and I prayed and asked God for help: "God, if this relationship is right for me, keep them here. If not, remove them."

A simple statement. Straight to the point. God appreciates clear prayers (John 15:7). Being direct is okay with Him. I was so desperate for peace of mind and freedom from the stress of my life that I was pushed toward Him as a last resort. Until that moment, I trusted my own abilities to problem-solve through emotional intelligence and intuition. Truthfully, I also couldn't think of a time that my self-reliance had failed me. This was my first moment of complete loss when seeking a clear next step. That was when I turned to the CEO who cannot fail. Looking back, I know God wants you and me to turn to Him before we reach those breaking points.

This story of my past reminds me to thank God for never giving up on me even in my darkest days. I believe you can thank God for the same thing in your life. As that relationship's season ended, I found my comfort in God. When my emotions bounced back and forth to the endpoints of sadness and peace, I prayed that prayer every day—sometimes feeling victorious and other times with tears in my eyes. The journey to end that season marked a formative experience for building my trust in Him. I learned God should own positioning the people in my life because He's much better at it than I am, so I continued the prayer for all my relationships—a significant other, friends, and colleagues.

Today, that two-sentence prayer is common in my conversations with God—surprisingly, often with regard to colleagues and business teams. In the professional realm, relationships create opportunity and contribute to overall fulfillment in the workplace. Relationships at work serve a variety of purposes: career development, mentorship, social networking, and upward mobility. Within the variety, there are pitfalls to avoid. You can accidentally become absorbed in the social benefits of work relationships—finally receiving an invite out to lunch with the "cool" people in the office, a notable win. However, you should not become distracted on the quest for comradery at the expense of establishing productive God-led relationships.

Colleagues can boost or block your career progression by impeding your path of Godliness. In professional places, people are generally on their best behavior, so at first, it may seem difficult to gain an understanding of a colleague's character and ethics. Contrary to that idea, there are moments for individuals to reveal their true characters—what brings them humor, what emotions they seek to evoke from others, what type of casual conversations they prefer to engage in. Rather than waiting for the moment, you should ask God for awareness when the character is revealed, along with guidance for those with whom to invest your time.

Let's consider the personalities on your business team today. Is there someone who rubs you the wrong way and you're not sure exactly why? Or someone who starts each day with an update on the latest gossip, news headline, or trending social media topic that always leaves you feeling stressed? Take notice of the changes in energy and mood when other people enter and exit your space. Be careful to protect the energy around you.

As you interact with your colleagues, ask God to let His spirit flood the room and to guard your eyes, ears, and heart against disillusions of the world. As you determine who stays in your circle and who should be temporarily passing through, rely on God to be the filter. After you ask, listen and be obedient to His instruction. Believe that He has the highest level of influence over your environment and the people in it.

Pray to God to position the right people around you at work and continue that prayer as your career expands into people-management. Be mindful that the "right people" does not simply mean people who share your perspective on all things. Instead, appreciate professional relationships that challenge you to improve, become more accurate, and stretch and grow at a faster pace than you would otherwise (Proverbs 27:17).

No matter where your career is today, you should develop habits that build a productive routine that you will maintain through the seasons of professional growth that God has for you. For example, you may start as an entry-level individual contributor, move into people management, move to higher levels of executive management, and become a senior leader, owner, or partner within the company. Each stage requires God-led relationships to flourish and negative people to be removed. Develop the habit of turning to God to shift people in and out of your life as necessary without malice, but instead with Godly love for them all (Matthew 5:44).

At an early age in corporate America, I earned the opportunity to have a startup idea funded by an executive in my company. I was in awe of the task to build my own team from scratch, manage people for the first time, and build and launch an idea that existed primarily in my mind. It was a rare and humbling experience to receive such an elevated vote of confidence.

That vote also came with internal pressure to perform and produce the results I convinced this executive that I was capable to produce. In what felt like the blink of an eye, gone were the days of joining a team, receiving a "how to" manual with clear goals based on previous business performance. Instead, I had the opportunity to bring an idea to life with the help of the talented colleagues I was responsible to hire. Let me summarize my feelings: "Okay, God, here we go!"

This was a huge step for me. A career-defining moment at a leading tech company. It was a moment many business people would describe as "too big to fail." It was growth opportunity into people management and on a new business program without an established team or process, so there was a lot changing at once. As I was getting started in the early weeks, I felt shocked and honored but confident.

Then, a few weeks later, I lost my focus on God as my CEO, and those feelings quickly transformed into fear and nervousness. I didn't want to let anyone down. I recall during a moment of prayer—maybe praise and worship—when it hit me: God is my CEO and He cannot fail. In that split second, I reminded myself for whom I work. My responsibilities are to listen to His guidance and not quit.

How to make that idea a reality came through my promise to remain disciplined, diligent, and relentlessly focused on God in both my new business experience and my prayer life. From then on, I turned to God for guidance and discernment as I was introduced to potential team members. I asked specifically for wisdom to hire people who would work well together in pursuit of the team's vision (Matthew 7:16-20).

The Church is called the Body of Christ (1 Corinthians 12:12-14). Although the body is one, it is made up of many parts working together. Before I unpack what that means for you as a Christian, let's take a moment to appreciate the complexities of the human body. The human body has more than ten unique systems that function simultaneously in a healthy body, a long list of hundreds of cell types required for those systems to function, and a detailed bone structure ranging in sizes and shapes that fit together perfectly. All these pieces, as diverse as they are, have a specific purpose and need to be in place and functioning in order for that body to operate as designed. There is both unity and diversity in the body.

Consider that you are a piece of Christ that has an integral purpose to His body. Your placement, health, and strengths are unique to you, and maintaining your purpose is required for Christ to function properly.

Now consider your circles of friends and colleagues as systems that impact the health and functionality of your body. How are they functioning? How are the pieces contributing? Is the right side overcompensating for a deficiency on the left side? Sure, injuries happen, but healing and rebuilding cannot be ignored in the human body.

The same should be true for your relationship circles. When you apply this logic to colleagues, you will shift away from viewing colleagues as laborers in a position to get a job done. Instead, you will see colleagues as teammates, each individual representing an important piece of the total, and each representing a relationship for you to be actively engaged in, committed to, and kept healthy.

With that perspective, you should then understand the importance of a strong start when building a team. The beginning matters because the environment you build is what will be cultivated and further defined and maintained by the people in it.

Desire a productive, diverse, good-spirited group of people to build relationships with. Make your asks and expectations clear to God regarding the relationships you have at work. In a twenty-four-hour day, generally you sleep for eight hours, work for eight hours, and free time for eight hours. So, approximately one-third of your day is spent with colleagues.

Now consider your prayer life. You likely pray for other people with whom you share your home and for friends and family with whom you spend free time, but what about the other third? Do you pray about relationships with colleagues? You should.

If you're an individual contributor, be selective about the team and manager you work with. Once you are placed on a team, be an influential member of the environment regardless of your title or level of experience. Remind yourself you were hired because of the skills and perspective you bring to the group; it's important to resist the temptation of comparison. Do not compare yourself to others or conform to negative moods of the team. You are uniquely called to be you, and who you are is independent of those in your surroundings. You are a meaningful piece of the body as you are. Do not try to take on a new form. Be yourself as God has created you.

As a manager, when building your own team, take it seriously. Write down the type of environment you will create. Be specific and include team-building activities you will establish—traditions and celebrations you will implement with high regard. Then remain intentional about meeting those objectives throughout the interview process.

Do not mistakenly optimize for speed at the expense of quality and fit. Instead, be patient as you identify strong individuals who also come together to offer a diverse mix of personalities and skillsets. Be careful to not hire the same strengths, as we know a variety of components matters to a fully functional and capable body. You will need diverse members to make up a highly functional team. Be sure to continuously turn to God and ask Him to reveal the right people for your organization, which includes people to add and people to let go.

Focus Scriptures

Read these scriptures to be reminded of how to ask God to manage the relationships in your life.

John 15:7 *If you remain in me and my words remain in you, ask whatever you wish, and it will be done for you.*

Matthew 7:16-20 *By their fruit you will recognize them. Do people pick grapes from thornbushes, or figs from thistles? Likewise, every good tree bears good fruit, but a bad tree bears bad fruit. A good tree cannot bear bad fruit, and a bad tree cannot bear good fruit. Every tree that does not bear good fruit is cut down and thrown into the fire. Thus, by their fruit you will recognize them.*

1 Corinthians 12:12-14 *Just as a body, though one, has many parts, but all its many parts form one body, so it is with Christ. For we were all baptized by one Spirit so as to form one body—whether Jews or Gentiles, slave or free—and we were all given the one Spirit to drink. Even so the body is not made up of one part but of many.*

Proverbs 27:17 *As iron sharpens iron, so one person sharpens another.*

Matthew 5:44 *But I tell you, love your enemies and pray for those who persecute you.*

Confession

Recite this prayer out loud when praying to ask God to manage the relationships in your life.

God, if this relationship is right for me, keep them here. If not, remove them. I ask for Your hand in the placement of the teammates, peers, managers, and mentors at work. I trust that You will remove those with ill will toward me and that You will continue to place me in the right environment with the perfect opportunities. I pray for Your favor with others and for wisdom to navigate the challenging spaces at work.

I pray that as I become a better leader that I carry forward the ability to discern who is for me from who is against me. When someone is removed, I will be thankful. When someone arrives, I will again be thankful. Both are blessings because I know You are in control of the relationships in my life. With God for me, who can be against me? With this prayer, I accept the movement and changes that occur in accordance with Your will.

I will walk into new relationships trusting You to guide my steps. I will say goodbye to those You remove, without grasping sadness or diminished growth by holding memories of the past. Instead, I will move forward in anticipation of the bigger and better things to come. Father, plant me in a work environment around colleagues and mentors with whom I will thrive. Let me give life to the environments I'm in and the people I influence.

Chapter 4

Keep your joy no matter the circumstances.

Growing up with siblings was awesome. When I look back on my childhood, I realize I learned fundamental communication skills and emotional intelligence while at home with my family. I am the third of four girls. As a teenager, one of my sisters would sometimes come home from school and announce to me, "I have an attitude, so don't talk to me." Being the younger sibling, I knew to leave her alone as requested *or else.*

Unknowingly, she was also teaching me that emotions can control your response to people if you allow it to happen. That lesson is one I learned to process through understanding God's love. Today, I can now articulate what was actually happening within her. She offered up full submission to her emotions, giving them dominance over her life, and unfortunately, mine too as I enabled it by fearfully accepting her request.

Thankfully, she has grown up and matured in her emotional reactions, and I have grown in my relationship as an heir with Christ to understand how to graciously disagree with people I love who are making wrong choices. Rather than agree with a misguided declaration in an effort to avoid conflict, I respectfully challenge with a biblical principle in an effort to expand their minds. Failure to do so will result in your mood shifting at the whims of other people and circumstances. In such instances, allowing emotional responses to dominate your behavior comes at the expense of other priorities.

In this childhood example, if I had the knowledge and courage to offer a counter-argument to my older sister, I would have advised her to guard her response to emotions and recognize when she was distracted from a productive objective.

In the professional realm, it is not uncommon to see adults respond to emotions as did my teenage sister—the highs can take you to incredible celebratory moments, and the lows hit hard and can pull you down to rock-bottom moments of devastation. It is unfortunate to experience recurring whiplash caused by an emotional rollercoaster.

At the office, the highs and lows in your mood or demeanor can be dictated by the latest business performance, manager approval, peer acceptance, or perceived visibility on a project. This is a dangerous space to operate within because it leaves you seeking validation from colleagues rather than understanding your own self-worth and your true source of prosperity in the Father. To overcome this pitfall, you must internalize the message of God's joy and relentlessly pursue it. When you develop the trust of God's explanation of joy (Proverbs 17:22) as a medicine for your heart and its role in your life, you will find yourself to be more emotionally stable. He is your source of peace and joy (James 1:2-3).

With this foundation, it is easier to rise above the emotions and maintain a Christ-like mood, temper, and disposition even when encountering the chaos and disappointments present in your world.

If you aren't sure how much the events in your workplace impact your mood outside of the office, try this exercise. Consider the amount of energy you spend complaining about work when you are away from the office or how long you are upset when you receive a bad report.

The Bible instructs you and me to finish the day with joy over our dinner because He has everything under control (Ecclesiastes 9:7). Is that true in your life? After that bad report, do you experience minutes, hours, or even days of emotional instability? If so, it is important to discover and apply a method that will shorten the unstable timeframe.

I have a strategy I use to reduce emotional turmoil. In those disappointing moments, I recommend you take three actions:

1. Turn to God; fix your mind on Him;

2. Recall your place in the world as His child; and

3. Ask Him to let there be more of Him and less of you.

The first action to "turn to God" may look slightly different for you; however, the common thread is that you choose to quiet your thoughts and listen for God. That may be done through silent prayer, out loud prayer in the Holy Spirit, singing along with worship music, or reading a Bible verse to clear your mind. Find your method to engage God and put it into action when you need to return to emotional stability.

Next, when you recall your place in the world as God has positioned you, it will remove the pressure to perform to a role or title in the work-place. No title is more powerful or important to your life than Child of God. The vastness of that title will make the disappointment of the moment shrink in significance.

Lastly, with boldness and vulnerability, ask for more of Him and less of you in your life. Remember, He knows what should and will happen next for you. Challenges at work and in your personal life can feel overwhelming if you believe you are alone to solve them. The good news is that you are not. He already knows how to overcome the toughest hurdles you will ever be presented with, and He's always with you. During this final step of emotional recovery, truly believe in your heart that your God makes a way when there is no way. When you release the heaviness of professional or personal disappointments to God, you should feel lighter. Give it to Him and listen to His guidance with joy in your heart.

As I became more comfortable turning to God during frustrating moments at work or after meetings that didn't go as well as planned, I noticed I'd bounce back to my joyful disposition much quicker and that the process became easier over time. I no longer internalized so much negativity about the things I couldn't control.

This three-step method will change your response to things that used to frustrate you. When you choose to reflect God in your daily response to the things of this world, you will receive the strength and joy He gives you, along with a more calm and peaceful demeanor because of your trust in Him.

In Matthew 8, Jesus is on a boat with His disciples and they are caught in a storm with high winds and rough waters. The men on the boat reach a level of panic and concern that led them to wake Jesus from His sleep. They are yelling for Him to help before it's too late and the boat is capsized. Jesus calmly awakens and says three simple words to calm the seas, "Peace, be still," and the waters became smooth in an instant. That same spirit that calmed the storm lives in you. He is your Father, your CEO, and He gives you His joy to keep you full. The fullness He offers you includes believing in His promise to make all things new (Psalm 46:1-2).

Yes, you will experience disappointment, discouragement, and sadness. And it is okay to have an emotional reaction to those experiences. Even Jesus wept—once for the people who rejected Him (Luke 19:41) and again when Lazarus died (John 11:35), so that should make you feel comfortable with having emotions. The difference between someone in a relationship with God and one who does not yet know Him is the impact obstacles have on their lives. With God as your CEO, when workdays or outcomes are challenging, you will not become severely weakened or build up diminishing thoughts about yourself and your abilities. Instead, you will be renewed through Him again and again, and that trust is where your confidence comes from during the storms.

As you excel and gain responsibilities at work, the circumstances of stress and worry increase as well. You must be careful not to subconsciously carry that stress with you throughout the workday and into your personal life. I celebrated when I made the transition from an individual contributor to a team manager, excited for the opportunity to lead people and show myself as a strong leader. This was the increase I had been praying for!

Looking back, I can now admit I seriously underestimated the expanded dimensions of my workload that would accompany this increase. There were days early on that I felt a heavy burden to live up to everyone's expectations and was bogged down by my own uncertainty. When I lacked clarity, it frustrated me in a new way because I wanted to shield my team from my vulnerability. It took a conscious effort, multiple times per day, to push myself into a state of mental and spiritual strength, positivity, and joy.

Thankfully, I already had a method to stabilize myself emotionally. That's why it is important for you to build habits and become faithful as early as possible to establish the norms for your life and the problem-solving strategies that work well for you. It is written that the devil comes to steal, kill, and destroy (John 10:10). During that period, my feelings of frustration were not of God, so I fixed my mind on Him as quickly as possible. The mind is powerful, and you control what you concentrate on. It is your responsibility to ensure your mental health. With God at the center, your mind will be stable and joy will be found in you.

The three-step process should be a framework to gather yourself and realign with your soul's CEO.

With practice, you will personalize it and get down to what works well for you and your relationship with Him. For myself, as I continued to refine my process, I discovered a way to open my heart to God's joy and calmness in an instant with a go-to vision.

When I feel stressed, frustrated, overwhelmed and joy is the furthest feeling from me, then I have my go-to vision to place God immediately at the center of it all. It may seem silly or trite, but as I stated, the mind is very powerful. I close my eyes and imagine lying under the sun by the ocean, the perfect breeze flowing over me, while God holds me in his hands as if they were a hammock. The visualization of God's hands as my hammock reminds me that He is my comforter and protector. It immediately brings a sense of calmness to my reality and a smile to my face. That simple visual reminds me how much I trust Him. His hands are there to support me every time. What a blessing to know He's always there for you and me to rest in.

I first saw that vision of calmness and joy during a prayer night at my church. It was amid a stressful season at work because I was having a hard time finding a new role within the company. In my career, when you want to change roles within the company, you set up "coffee chats" around various departments to find your new best-fitting team and opportunity. Sounds ideal because you're the captain of your fate, but it can quickly become daunting when you feel like no role is really designed for you. I found myself doubting my goals and considering settling for a role that did not meet my standards because it was attainable.

You may have also experienced a point of discouragement that caused you to consider settling. My mind was in self-doubt, and I was sometimes visibly frustrated at work and outwardly unhappy in private conversations with my mentor. The prayer night was on the perfect day for me.

As I worshiped and prayed, I imagined being rescued by Him and the hammock vision came to mind. "A joyful heart is a good medicine, but a crushed spirit dries up the bones" (Proverbs 17:22). My heart was in disarray from floundering at work. His joy calmed it all.

That has been my go-to vision for years now. It works for my relationship with Him, as it reminds me that He guided me to victory then and He will do it again.

I encourage you to find a go-to vision that works for you.

Focus Scriptures

Read these scriptures to be reminded of how to keep your joy no matter the circumstances.

Proverbs 17:22 *A cheerful heart is good medicine, but a crushed spirit dries up the bones.*

James 1:2-4 *Consider it pure joy, my brothers and sisters, whenever you face trials of many kinds, because you know that the testing of your faith produces perseverance. Let perseverance finish its work so that you may be mature and complete, not lacking anything.*

Ecclesiastes 9:7 *Go, eat your food with gladness, and drink your wine with a joyful heart, for God has already approved what you do.*

Psalm 46:1-2 *God is our refuge and strength, an ever-present help in trouble. Therefore we will not fear, though the earth give way and the mountains fall into the heart of the sea.*

John 15:11 *I have told you this so that my joy may be in you and that your joy may be complete.*

Romans 14:17 *For the kingdom of God is not a matter of eating and drinking, but of righteousness, peace and joy in the Holy Spirit.*

Galatians 5:22-23 *But the fruit of the Spirit is love, joy, peace, forbearance, kindness, goodness, faithfulness, gentleness and self-control. Against such things there is no law.*

Confession

Recite this prayer out loud when praying to ask God to keep your joy no matter the circumstances.

God, Your word says joy is like a medicine.

Father, I come to You to find Your joy and peace in this moment, and in every moment, let me trust that You are relentless in your comfort and support. I will fix my eyes and heart on You in spite of all circumstances. You are an everlasting and never-changing God, and I know I can count on Your joy in my life forever. Turn my trial into my testimony, Father. I will not plant myself deep in self-doubt, sadness, or darkness. I will move forward in pursuit of Your strength, joy, and peace. God, continue to reveal Your joy in my heart and in my life. Thank you for speaking to me and empowering me to reflect Your joy back into my world daily.

Chapter 5

Seek advisors with a proven track record of success.

Mentors matter. The Bible teaches the importance of advisors throughout the text, especially in the book of Proverbs. "The way of fools seems right to them, but the wise listen to advice" (Proverbs 12:15). It is important that you seek wise counsel, which is one of my favorite instructions in the Bible because it is so straightforward. I appreciate when there is little room for misinterpretation or misunderstanding.

Let's break down the paraphrase to seek wise counsel. First, "seek" is defined as *the desire to obtain or achieve.* Second, "wise" is defined as *having or showing experience, knowledge, and good judgment.* Lastly, "counsel" is defined as *advice, especially that given formally.* To connect those three definitions, you can conclude that we are to obtain formal advice from those who have shown good judgment.

The book of Proverbs emphasizes the role of advisors is to provide guidance and wisdom that will help you surmount obstacles and avoid error. Advisors are helpful to share ideas and challenges with because the conversation can affirm your point of view or prevent you from making incorrect decisions. It is beneficial to have someone who will ask you "why" a few times to ensure you have thoughtfully considered the scenarios before you.

As you seek advisors and mentors for professional development, resist the temptation to conflate tenure with wisdom. Years of experience does not necessarily correlate with good judgment, ethics, or business instincts. Do away with time as your measure. Instead, look for the individual with a track record of success and a welcoming spirit because that record will certainly accompany the wise. This may be the opposite of what you'd assume early in your career when you often look for people who have been around the longest to be the best teachers. Do your best to reject the norm, ignore the constructs of time and tenure, and focus your mentor selection criteria on results and good judgment.

It is beneficial to have a group of advisors you can turn to for different areas of feedback or for a variety of perspectives on the same area of your career. As you navigate professionally, you should aim to have a handful of advisors and mentors with diverse backgrounds and accomplishments because the types of challenges you face will change. The life stage you're moving into will also change, so you'll benefit from the wisdom of people who can help you see around the corners and ahead of those changes.

Each mentor should have a different story, ideally resulting in a range of strengths that you can hone in on when necessary. Diversity of thought is important to productive professional mentorship, especially when it comes to creative problem-solving and idea-generating. Without counsel, plans fail, but with many advisers, they succeed (Proverbs 15:22).

At work, when you reach a roadblock it's great to have people with whom you can bounce off ideas and challenge your perspective. Those types of conversations I refer to as "development debates" have helped me build up the strength of my position on a subject or brought me into a new thought as ideas are batted back and forth.

In the past six years, I've had two career navigation advisors with distinctly opposing styles. The first was someone who asked to mentor me. I was honored to be considered, so I agreed. Truthfully, I had no idea how to find a mentor, and I didn't want to throw my name into a hat for a random match, so being asked by a colleague I had a good rapport with was ideal. We planned to meet monthly for one hour to talk about work and career topics. We often met over lunch for a casual conversation—no notes, no follow-ups from the prior month. In fact, we talked often about sports, travel, and the people we knew in common; work was the least recurring topic of conversation. It felt more like catching up with a buddy than an advisor. I was okay with that because I didn't know any better.

Today, I'd describe it as a blessing that the mentor relocated and was unable to continue the mentorship. That inspired me to think about what an advisor should be and what I wanted out of a mentor relationship. I thought about Proverbs 11:14, "For lack of guidance a nation falls, but victory is won through many advisers."

I prayed to be pointed in the direction of wisdom toward career navigation because that was the primary decision facing me at that time. It was that lens of wisdom that led me to reach out to a senior member within my company for mentorship. We had a foundational level of familiarity, as I was one of over one hundred people in her organization. She was a VP, so our familiarity was valuable—she knew my name and we had talked several times in the past though not much beyond casual chats.

When I reached out for mentorship, I sent a detailed email that was professional and concise. It included what I wanted to learn from her and my near-term career goals at the company. With such a high level of respect for her time and authority, I was nervous if she'd even respond to my email let alone accept the ask. Prayerfully, I did not let doubt prevent me from pursuing the mentorship. I sent the note.

When she agreed, it showed she considered me worth her time. In advance of our first meeting, I knew it was important to prepare as a sign of appreciation of her investment in me. During that first meeting, I brought a list of my strengths and accomplishments thus far at the company, what I was looking for in my next role, and where I'd like to focus my professional growth. To be honest, that single meeting involved more preparation than the total of two years with my previous mentor because I valued her wisdom and perspective. When you are in the presence of wise people, it raises your expectations of yourself. No one had to tell me to prepare more because I was meeting with a vice president. Instead, I knew to raise my personal standards because of the value of her time, and it brought out a capability in me I hadn't known I possessed.

At the beginning of our mentorship, I was nervous to expose areas of weakness with this mentor so, instead, I focused on sharing my most confident ideas to ask for her perspective. As we built professional trust, I began to share ideas that were less developed to co-create with her feedback in real time.

Today, I confidently go to her with tough decisions and key problems to solve, not specifically for the answer but because I am interested in learning her process of thinking through scenarios to help me improve. She provides me with frameworks for decision-making, and sometimes we whiteboard ideas and solutions on the spot. There are bumps in the road and opposing points of view as we move through subjects, but my respect for her wisdom and the attention she pays to dissect my process has cultivated a balanced dialogue between us. I am confident her mentorship has pushed me miles ahead as a leader and professional.

Now, several years into our mentorship relationship, I confidently understand the value of being sharpened by those close to you. Iron sharpens iron, and one man sharpens another (Proverbs 27:17). You should seek those who will sharpen you and keep them close in your life. It can be easier to surround ourselves with people who look like us, talk like us, and think like us, but that can limit your growth. Be careful to pursue growth, not exclusively comfort, in the relationships you invest in.

I recall the first piece of critical advice that mentor shared with me in the early stages when I was searching for a new role in the company. To provide more context, I believed my current role had run its course and decided my ideal new role would be one that essentially changed every area of my career. I wanted to change functions, business type, and scope of responsibility. Did my resume clearly indicate I was capable of what I desired? No, not directly. It was a stretch, and any manager who hired me would be taking a risk believing in my potential without one hundred percent transferrable accomplishments on my resume.

This meant the process of finding a new role was slower than my previous experiences when I had moved along within more related fields or businesses. That slow pace was frustrating. In a meeting about this issue, the mentor said, "Don't run from a role. Run to a role." That simple statement sharpened my commitment and inspired me to believe it would happen for me.

Although it took seven months to find a manager willing to take that risk, I am grateful that patience and confidence led me rather than fear. That decision came from wise counsel.

While this one mentoring relationship had many benefits to my professional growth, she was numbered mentor number one on my mentor team, which I have spent years developing. Today, I have four formal mentors and even more informal advisors for professional growth and overall well-being. My mentor team keeps me accountable to my goals and standards, offers course correction, and challenges my mind with alternative perspectives. You cannot overlook the importance of a team of mentors. These relationships should be filled with passionate conversations that lead you to discover more about yourself and provide tangible strategies to pursue your vision.

When I consider someone as a potential mentor, I pray about it first and listen to God. You should consider this approach as well. The people whom you grant influence over your life should be God-chosen people. It is not enough to seek mentorship from someone with accomplishments and a prestigious title; you should also find out what leads and motivates them. Are they spiritually grounded? Do they celebrate others or bring people down? Do they manage their authority with grace or with fear tactics? These are questions you should consider and evaluate before planting someone in your life as a mentor.

Also, recognize mentors are not the same as friends. While the two are not mutually exclusive, often it is beneficial to have a friendship boundary to maximize the mentorship relationship at the beginning. As the mentorship evolves, if a closer friendship naturally develops, that is okay but not a necessary goal.

The Bible also tells us to be a vessel (2 Timothy 2:21; 2 Corinthians 4:6-7). What God pours into us, let us then pour it out on our world. That principle applies to mentorship. Eventually, you should aim to become a professional mentor to others as your own career develops.

Can you imagine hundreds of thousands of God-led business leaders across the world being the greatest mentors in their companies? How would that change company cultures and business dynamics? You should commit to being wise counsel to others in your sphere of influence, including those who are not yet Christian who will also seek your guidance and wisdom. Your professional mentorship could lead that person to God, which is your greatest calling. Allow yourself to become a vessel in your professional environment.

To be a mentor can feel exciting at first and then shift to become burdensome if you let it. I approach mentorship opportunities with a simple system. First, you must know your capacity for mentorship relationships, and do not take on more than you can fit into your schedule. Yes, it should feel like an honor that someone trusts you to influence his or her career. However, a sign of wisdom is to know what offers to accept and which to respectfully decline.

Next, when you enter a mentor relationship, be upfront about the rules of engagement. It is okay to establish standards and expectations for your time so both people understand the expected investment. For example, the VP mentor I previously described immediately put me in touch with her assistant for scheduling. She informed me of the meeting frequency and that meetings would always take place in her office. The small detail of the location at her office as compared to my previous lunch cafeteria mentor set a tone for expectations.

Lastly, as you mentor multiple people at various stages of their careers, be mindful that no two people are the same. Avoid common pitfalls of only mentoring people who remind you of yourself or comparing your mentees to one another. In the same way that you benefit from diverse thought amongst mentors, you will also benefit from a diverse set of mentees because they'll have different ways to communicate, receive feedback, and process information. Your ability to embrace these differences will make you better at understanding people.

With the diverse personalities, be careful to avoid comparisons because it can be detrimental to meeting the needs of your mentee. With God as your CEO, the mentor and mentee teams in your life should be filtered through Him. As I previously shared, He places people in your life with purpose. Identify the wise and know when you have wisdom to impart to others. Enter those spaces with intentionality and you will experience exponential growth from mentorship.

Focus Scriptures

Read these scriptures to be reminded of how to ask God to seek advisors with a proven track record of success.

Proverbs 12:15 *The way of fools seems right to them, but the wise listen to advice.*

Proverbs 15:22 *Plans fail for lack of counsel, but with many advisers they succeed.*

Proverbs 11:14 *For lack of guidance a nation falls, but victory is won through many advisers.*

Proverbs 27:17 *As iron sharpens iron, so one person sharpens another.*

2 Timothy 2:21 *Those who cleanse themselves from the latter will be instruments for special purposes, made holy, useful to the Master and prepared to do any good work.*

2 Corinthians 4:6-7 *For God, who said, "Let light shine out of darkness," made his light shine in our hearts to give us the light of the knowledge of God's glory displayed in the face of Christ. But we have this treasure in jars of clay to show that this all-surpassing power is from God and not from us.*

Confession

Recite this prayer out loud when praying to ask God to seek advisors with a proven track record of success.

God, I pray for guidance in my career from those who are also led by You. I seek relationships with mentors and advisors who will sharpen me, challenge me, and steer me in the right direction. I welcome difficult conversations from the wise.

Give me the wisdom to separate opinions meant to distract from those meant to develop me. As I grow, God, give me the ability to invest in others as an advisor as well. Continue to use me as a vessel of Your love, wisdom, and grace on a daily basis. Thank you for positioning the right influences along my path.

Chapter 6

Make claim of yourself as a problem solver.

As a Child of God, you should believe that you are made in His image. Thus, you must also believe that you are a creator because He is a creator.

Who is the greatest inventor in the history of the world? The greatest engineer in the history of the world? The greatest botanist? The greatest painter? Take a moment to look at the results from our God, and the answer is obvious every time. As an heir of Jesus, that creativity and ability to make things new in your world are also within you. It is your responsibility to remove the limitations of the current state of the business or state of the world and push yourself to become a creative problem-solver by seeking and listening to God.

To be creative is vulnerable. The fear of rejection or failure is magnified when the creation is from you because the rejection feels more personal. A common and relatable example of this happens at potlucks. Imagine you are responsible for bringing the dessert. When you bring a store-bought dessert and people don't like it, you can assign the failure to the store or the staff. But if it's a homemade dessert and people don't like it, you defend the dessert more or you question the judgment of the party.

That fear of personal failure can lead you to seek perfection before ever sharing your creation with others, which unfortunately leaves people to be idea-generators but not doers. It is disappointing to be filled with ideas but without action. To avoid this pitfall, trust God to fill in the gaps between what you know today and your goals for tomorrow. Then get started and allow Him guide you. Don't wait for perfection. (II Corinthians 12:9-11).

I keep a note in my phone of ideas. Over the years, I've captured a variety of ideas—businesses, products, apps, experiences—that I read over regularly. One of those ideas led me to write this book. Admittedly, I used many reasons to disqualify myself from being an author before I ever started. I had a clear motivation for the final result, but I had no experience from a book-writing course, nor did I have an outline for the book or contact with an editor. The mystery of the unknown scared me.

Nonetheless, one day I began writing. As I embarked on the process, the outline came together, friends with relevant experience became volunteer editors and cover art designers, and scriptures were recalled and sought after. Several people who provided their guidance and talents to help me get this book into your hands were people I did not know when I first started writing and were placed in my path only after I took action. That is how I know it was God who filled in the gaps to complete this vision. He was able to do His part because I trusted Him enough to start.

In your job, this creativity may not be a new product or experience, but it could be an innovative solution to a recurring problem or a new business strategy for your industry that unlocks an opportunity for the company.

However, the process begins the same way:

1. Capture all your ideas, big and small;

2. Review them and see which one(s) stand out most prominently to you;

3. Imagine what the world would look like after the idea is complete; and

4. Start expanding on the idea, talk to people about it, find motivation to get started.

These are the steps for starting the process, not an exhaustive list of a complete process because the most important part is starting. Also, the complete process differs dramatically based on what you pursue.

If in your adult life you do not describe yourself as a creative person, think back to your childhood. Children draw unrecognizable lines and shapes. Children make up games with some of most complex rules and scorekeeping logic. Children imagine entire atmospheres and creatures that no one else has thought of. You were that child. I was too.

As you grow up, fears, failures, and rejections of life may have caused you to create walls of self-preservation. When you are hurt, you avoid repeating that action to avoid the pain. It can be conscious or subconscious; either way, that avoidance can contribute to you burying your creativity due to fear.

Release those fears, remind yourself you are called to be a creator, and allow your imagination to produce something from your mind. Beginning each day with that perspective makes my business challenges as a product manager more solvable because it removes many of the constraints in my thinking. When you hit a roadblock—not if, but when—remember to call on God for solutions and to reveal the next steps. "God gives us power to get wealth" (Deuteronomy 8:18), and wealth often comes through professional success. Therefore, our power to achieve professional success comes through God.

Believe in His guidance as you navigate the issues closest to your role in the company and when you hear of other business problems that you may have ideas to solve. To get into this mindset of creative problem-solving means to question current processes and try to imagine a different future. If you can see the end of a new idea—how it will impact the company, what customers will have to say about it, where else it can be applied—you are a dreamer and one step closer to being a creator. Do not build ideas based on the current resources or current constraints. Instead, consider them later in the process to determine what tradeoffs can be made and which things are non-negotiable.

Beyond ideas that will benefit your company, you may also uncover entrepreneurial ideas and solutions to your day-to-day life. It is exciting to have an idea you are passionate about, and that excitement usually leads you to share the idea with someone close to you. Be prepared to experience rejection when you take the risk of being a creator, even among those you consider close friends or family. Rather than feeling instant defeat, trust in God's instruction and allow your response to be led by Him. Remind yourself, "[His] word is a lamp for my feet and a light on my path" (Psalm 119:105).

If your spirit is guiding you toward this entrepreneurial idea or solution, push yourself to pursue it. Think about why it was rejected. It could be that the idea was not presented to the right person or that it was not ready to be shared at all.

You will need perseverance and thick skin to be creative because people challenge what they do not yet understand, and people who know you well may find it difficult to imagine you doing something big and beyond what you are known for. I encourage you to be okay with opposition from those who cannot receive your ideas due to constraints in their minds. Be careful to share new and vulnerable ideas with other dreamers and creators. Find a community within your company or your peers that believe in the fruitfulness of innovation. When you uncover an idea stirring within you, even without the support of the people you expect, be determined to start. Then ask God how, and it will be revealed in time (Matthew 7:7).

I shared my process for keeping ideas in a note on my phone. In the beginning, I used to write down ideas and not actually do anything about them. It was a fun list for me to reread and daydream about every now and then. It did not take other people to reject my creativity; sadly, I convinced myself I was not yet ready to create something on my own and enforced barriers. That changed when I internalized the affirmation, "I can do all this through him who gives me strength" (Philippians 4:13). With God as my CEO, my business is fully funded, well-resourced, and successful. The same is true for you. That verse says you and I can do all things, but you and I can miss the opportunity to see that reality in our lives because we never start doing.

To avoid being the person who finds joy in simply rereading the list of ideas, I recommend you grab hold of the power that comes from speaking your ideas out loud and making a real action plan. Do not wait for permission to start. Instead, write down your ideas as you imagine them today, and reread them often to listen for which ones stand out. Then, start to develop those standouts and let it continue to unfold, all while you keep your faith and abide in God to provide (John 15:5-6).

So often, we make the mistake of putting guardrails on our lives—waiting until we're ready, and by then, it will be too late. Even without visibility of the complete picture, you still move forward and take action, and then you are walking in faith. That also describes several examples of people receiving a miracle from Jesus. In John 2, when Jesus turns water into wine, it first required the people to obey Jesus and fill the large vessels with water, and then take a cup of the water to the host of the party and present it as wine. The beverage did not become wine until after it was en route to the host. In that miracle, taking action in faith was a prerequisite. I believe the same is true in your life as a creative problem-solver.

In your professional pursuits, do not be afraid to take actions of faith. Be led by God and be obedient, and then trust your CEO to show you the way. In this faith exercise, the part you can forget is that it requires work from you before you see the results. Do not sit stagnant while asking God to move mountains in your life. That is not the example that has been presented to us. Claim yourself to be a problem-solver by also proclaiming to be a doer. In your office, seek the reputation as one who gets the job done. You will be blessed to see the paths and doors that open when you have such a reputation.

Focus Scriptures

Read these scriptures to be reminded of how to ask God to make claim of yourself as a problem solver.

Deuteronomy 8:18 *But remember the Lord your God, for it is he who gives you the ability to produce wealth, and so confirms his covenant, which he swore to your ancestors, as it is today.*

Psalm 119:105 *Your word is a lamp for my feet, a light on my path.*

Matthew 7:7 *Ask and it will be given to you; seek and you will find; knock and the door will be opened to you.*

Philippians 4:13 *I can do all this through him who gives me strength.*

John 15:5-6 *I am the vine; you are the branches. If you remain in me and I in you, you will bear much fruit; apart from me you can do nothing. If you do not remain in me, you are like a branch that is thrown away and withers; such branches are picked up, thrown into the fire and burned.*

Confession

Recite this prayer out loud when praying to ask God to make claim of yourself as a problem solver.

Thank you for vision and passion, God. I believe the ideas from You are filled with purpose, and I will pursue them in faith. I will not be discouraged by obstacles in my work environment because I trust in You to help me identify new ideas and new solutions that will benefit my colleagues, company, and my reputation. As I pursue new ideas and experience the vulnerability, keep me grounded and encouraged through Your love. All things are possible through You. I am an heir with Jesus, made in Your image, and called to bring something unique into my world. I ask for obedience and discipline to pursue what You have designed for me.

Chapter 7

Develop a preparation routine for each day.

Start your day with God. The temptations of the world start as soon as your eyes open. Most people wake up and reach for their cell phones to scroll through emails or social media posts and find themselves already stressed about the day ahead. It can be subtle on some days, but be aware your enemy is constantly at work. Therefore, it is critical to pause at the start of your day to speak with your ultimate advisor and mentor, God. One of the keys of developing a God-centered morning routine is to discover your daily renewal process.

My favorite way to prepare for the day is to blast music—plain and simple, music is what motivates me to get moving most days. When I was in high school, I listened to my favorite rappers or R&B singers to get hyped for the day ahead. In my mid-twenties, as I grew closer to my Father, I listened to praise and worship music in the mornings, which changed my life. I started the habit after deciding to try a new routine of morning prayer.

The plan was to pray for five minutes before getting out of bed for work.

I started on a Monday, in my room in silence—I always prayed in the quiet—and began to pray and talk with God. After saying all the words I had for God and feeling accomplished, I checked the time and only about one minute had passed. Five minutes was going to be a struggle! To help the time pass, I added background worship music, so when I ran out of things to talk about, I would begin to join in and sing the worship songs to meet my goal of five minutes of prayer.

After five days of pushing through morning prayers with the help of the songs, I was relieved when it was finally Saturday. I had already decided weekend mornings would be different. I wasn't preparing myself for productivity or to be the professional version of myself, so I decided that meant I didn't need to begin with so much focus on connecting with God. On that Saturday morning, I was excited to turn on a playlist of my favorite hip-hop tracks, with the volume up high to kick-start my day as I'd done so many times before.

However, this time there was an unavoidable difference in my heart and mind. Immediately, my energy was restless. I skipped to the next song, hoping the next tune would be the right song to get me in the zone, but it didn't work. My ears—and my spirit—wanted praise and worship music. I skipped again about halfway through the second song. When the third song was also disappointing, I switched to worship music and felt content and happy. That may be one of the most vivid emotional contrasts I have ever felt. It is now my go-to reference to convey the difference between feeding my flesh and feeding my spirit (Galatians 5:16-17).

Five years into the prayer, praise, and worship morning routine, I am convinced nothing is better for my soul's relaxation and my mind's renewal each day. I can do this without problem for an hour on a Saturday morning, and I leave the house refreshed and ready to win.

Preparation is key to peak performance. You probably find it easier to accept that principle in the context of academics or athletics. If you study, you will do better on the test. If you train, you will do better in the competition. I urge you to not forget that this principle also applies when talking about your spirit. To prepare to be your best spiritual mind and presence each day, pray at the onset. Go to your Father and talk with Him about the day ahead, your goals for the week, and specific outcomes you believe in Him for. Share the early thoughts for ideas you hope to create and thank Him in advance for the problems you will solve that day. Build up your spirit and trust in your CEO through prayer and faith (Jude 20).

The other strategies I shared with you are practices to adopt during the day as you encounter people, places, and decision points. However, this strategy of preparation with God comes before all those moments and is foundational to the success of your professional pursuits. Start your day being reminded you are a Child of God and His gifts and blessings are here for you. That mindset will give you the strongest boost out of bed that you can imagine.

Beginning the day with God is for more than your benefit. You and I are called to be prepared to be protectors of those in the community around us (Ezekiel 38:7). My morning routine with God involves music. Your routine with Him may be different, and that's okay. The important part is that you commit to discovering how you best plug into His spirit. If you like to go for a run to start your day, consider praying out loud for one minute of your run or listening to the Bible in your headphones. If you usually read the news with a cup of coffee, consider prayer journaling for one page before reading the news.

Try a few things. Find what works best for you and stick to it. The days you deviate, your spirit will notice, and so will your mind. There is a method that will work for you, and when you discover it, it will change your life.

It became harder for me to be upset at drivers during my morning commute after an hour in prayer and worship with God. When I get frustrated behind the wheel, I am quicker to refocus my mind on God because I have already spent time with Him that day.

Prayer can be intimidating. I described how five minutes seemed like an eternity when I first started morning prayers, and now I can pray for thirty minutes without noticing the time. That evolution happened when I opened my heart to make my prayers about more than me.

One morning I tried a new strategy—pray for one person at a time. I started with my mom, then my dad, and then with each of my three sisters. Soon, I found myself praying out loud with everything I had within me because I believed in God for their lives. Sometimes I would tear up, and other times I would say a phrase that resonated and would repeat it a few times. The goal of five minutes of prayer had been unlocked for me, and I discovered my morning routine with God. I praise Him through song and enter into prayer out loud with intent and focus.

He already knows us and our hearts, but we are still required to open ourselves to Him. When you pray before a workday, start with a few points to help you get into a flow with God:

1. Thank Him for giving you another day to make an impact;

2. Pray over your schedule (remember chapter one);

3. Ask for protection and safety for you and your family;

4. Ask for an opportunity to bring His joy to someone; and

5. Surrender an insecurity, a problem you are dealing with.

When you commit yourself to be the Child of God, you will find yourself wanting to know Him and share yourself so He can know you. There is no place you'll find yourself that God hasn't experienced and already seen you through. In 1 John 1:9, we're called to confess our sins to Him, not because He needs to be updated on what happened in our lives, but because He needs to see our honesty, vulnerability, and trust in Him to forgive and cleanse us.

The above list of topics for morning prayer is in order of difficulty: easy to hard. After you start to develop a relationship with God and get to know Him, you will be able to surrender your whole self and let God into your heart completely. It takes trust, love, and understanding to surrender your weaknesses and shortcomings. Through habit-building and relationship-development with God, you will get to that place. As you listen to Him, you will also desire to be obedient because you trust His instruction is good and correct for your life.

Recall when you were a student. You probably experienced two types of teachers—one who knew the subject well and could give great examples and references, and another who read directly from the textbook because they didn't know details on the subject and found it difficult to answer questions or provide relatable examples.

God is a scholar of all subjects. If you don't understand the first time, look for another example in the Bible or ask Him to reveal the truth in another way. It's no coincidence that the four gospels retell the same stories from Matthew, Mark, Luke, and John. God wanted us to hear those stories from various vantage points to have a personal revelation that rings true in our own lives. A daily preparation routine that starts with God will guide you into a deeper relationship with Him, and it will remind you to call on Him throughout the day.

Your life will become a testimony of God's promises when you develop a loving relationship with Him. He will reveal all you need to succeed when you ask (James 1:5) because you are His child.

Focus Scriptures

Read these scriptures to be reminded of how to ask God to develop a preparation routine for each day.

Galatians 5:16-17 *So I say, walk by the Spirit, and you will not gratify the desires of the flesh. For the flesh desires what is contrary to the Spirit, and the Spirit what is contrary to the flesh. They are in conflict with each other, so that you are not to do whatever you want.*

Jude 20-21 *But you, dear friends, by building yourselves up in your most holy faith and praying in the Holy Spirit, keep yourselves in God's love as you wait for the mercy of our Lord Jesus Christ to bring you to eternal life.*

Ezekiel 38:7 *Get ready; be prepared, you and all the hordes gathered about you, and take command of them.*

James 1:5 *If any of you lacks wisdom, you should ask God, who gives generously to all without finding fault, and it will be given to you.*

Confession

Recite this prayer out loud when praying to ask God to develop a preparation routine for each day.

God, thank you for the gift of life. Thank you for the opportunity to continue to fulfill the calling You have for me. I pray that You reveal my purpose to me in Your own time, my steps are ordered, and I obediently follow You. I know there will be challenges and obstacles, and I can already say "thank you" for deliverance because Your strength lives in me. Let me be a blessing in my world today. Let my presence bring moments of peace and joy upon the lives of others. I am grateful to understand that this life is bigger than me, God. Let me be prepared to share the story of my savior and my testimony whenever I can with kindness and grace.

Endnotes

Pray for Potatoes is about understanding the most meaningful career title you will ever have as Child of God. He tells you to be on fire for Him, to be an atmosphere of boiling water in reflecting His love, grace, strength, and joy into our world. Then, concern yourself with the conditions of others. Pray their hearts will be softened for you and your spirit by believing potatoes will enter your boiling water, not eggs to be hardened by your presence.

When examining the condition of your own heart, first realize a Child of God gives their heart to Him completely. The condition of your heart impacts your life from the inside out, not simply in the literal sense as the engine of our bodies but spiritually. To keep a clean heart—a soft heart—you must renew your mind daily in Christ.

You and I should be thankful for God's relentless pursuit of our hearts because He pursued them even when we were sprinting away in the opposite direction. To let God into your heart is to give yourself to Him, surrender your own plans, and seek to achieve His plans above all else.

In the workplace, the people within your sphere of influence are placed there for a reason beyond their job description. God has planned an encounter for you, and that moment can be influenced by your preparation through God's word. When God is in your heart and you're in good spiritual condition, your work is not yet finished. His plan for your life is one of abundant success and fruitfulness that will serve as a testimony of His love and grace.

Trust God and develop habits that allow you to operate from a Godly state of mind professionally. It will change your life.

Meet the Author

Rovina Broomfield is passionate about God, business, and unwavering joy. She holds a master's in business administration from Olin Business School and an undergraduate degree in Finance from Washington University in St. Louis. She enjoys an exciting career in one of the largest tech companies in the world and has successfully launched businesses, both within her company and independently.

Her passions and career experiences combined to produce this book, as she desires to deliberately connect spirituality, leadership, and innovation for professionals.

Rovina attends Christian Faith church and lives in Seattle, Washington.

Connect with Rovina on social media
@rovinaciarra.

Made in the USA
San Bernardino, CA
05 December 2018